THE NEW COUNTRY

THE NEW COUNTRY

Abraham Shulman

CHARLES SCRIBNER'S SONS · NEW YORK

Frontispiece: Hester Street on New York's Lower East Side

Copyright © 1976 Abraham Shulman

Library of Congress Cataloging in Publication Data

Shulman, Abraham.
    The new country.

    1. Jews in New York (City)—Pictorial works. 2.
New York (City)—Description—Views. 3. United States
—Emigration and immigration. I. Title.
F128.9.J5S54   974.7'1'004924   76-15122
ISBN 0-684-14704-1

1 3 5 7 9 11 13 15 17 19 MD/C 20 18 16 14 12 10 8 6 4 2

Printed in the United States of America

CONTENTS

Acknowledgments   vii

Introduction   1

America in the Shtetl   55

The Exodus   61

Arrival   73

The New Land   81

Children   103

Work   115

Holidays   131

Old Age   151

Theater   165

Agricultural Settlements   177

Family Album   183

ACKNOWLEDGMENTS

Many of the photos in this book have been reproduced from the old files of the Sunday Illustrated supplement of the *Jewish Daily Forward.* Others come from the archives of the Yiddish Scientific Institute, YIWO; The Hebrew Immigrants Aid Society, HIAS; the Amalgamated Clothing Workers' Union; The International Ladies Garment Workers' Union, ILGWU; the Educational Alliance; the Bialystoker Nursing Home; Jewish Community Centers around the country; and private collections.

The author wishes to express his gratitude to all those who helped him in his work, particularly the Association of the *Jewish Daily Forward;* Mr. Marek Web of YIWO; Mr. Burt Beck of Amalgamated; Mr. Leon Stein of ILGWU; Mr. Raymond Gebiner of HIAS; Mr. Isaac Rybalowski of the Bialystoker Center; and Mr. E. Bashein of New York.

THE NEW COUNTRY

THE NEW COUNTRY

The overwhelming majority of the 6 million Jews who live in America today are descendants of the immigrants who came to this country from the shtetls, the small Jewish towns in Eastern Europe which existed for over six hundred years, until their destruction in World War II by the Germans. Over 2.5 million of those Jews came to America between 1880 and 1924, at which time immigration was restricted and practically halted for the people of Eastern and Southern Europe.

This book is principally a collection of photographs of those newly Americanized Jews, photos taken in the early years of this unprecedented mass exodus from the Eastern European bondage to the "Promised Land." It also contains a number of photos taken in the Old Country, at the place of bondage. What is striking in those photos taken on both sides of the Atlantic is that they are so very similar; in many cases it is hard to tell whether they were taken in the Old Country or in the New.

The street scenes of the Lower East Side in New York, with their hundreds of pushcarts lining the curbs, resemble the market place in any shtetl in Eastern Europe. The tenement houses look like slum sections of Jewish neighborhoods in the towns of Poland or Lithuania. Apartments with shabby furniture and crumbling walls, hung with portraits of bearded relatives, seem to be exact replicas of dwellings in the Old Country.

But the most remarkable similarities are found in the faces of the people. Old men with beards and sidelocks, women with kerchiefs wrapped around their *sheytls,* the traditional wigs worn by married women, photographed against the background of New York or Philadelphia, look exactly like their counterparts in Eastern Europe. Family members, grouped around worktables in apartments that have been transformed into workshops, gatherings of men and women in old age homes, youngsters carrying bundles of cloth, children playing in the streets, present images that could have been lifted directly from a family album of the Old Country.

The reasons for these similarities are simple: most of the people in these photos had arrived only recently from the shtetl. They had had little time for substantial change. Moreover, most of them had come to the New World determined, in a fundamental sense, to continue their old existence while, at the same time, becoming fully "Americanized." The two desires obviously were contradictory and mutually exclusive, but the unusual quality of these immigrants consisted precisely in the fact that for a very long time these two desires coexisted. Thus, the history of these Eastern European Jews is so extraordinary, and so very often misunderstood.

If we look closely at some of the photographs, we can already detect signs of nascent change. Some of the elderly men, for instance, still wear long black caftans and *Yiddish hitls* (the traditional visored Jewish black cloth caps), but in most cases the caftans have become shorter until they have acquired the length of the fashionable "Prince Albert" (called "Prince Isaac" by the immigrants), and the *Yiddish hitls* have given way to straw hats and derbies. Many women still wear shawls wrapped around their heads, but many more are already wearing elaborate hats. The poor and neglected clothes of the shtetl are disappearing. Even the pushcart peddlers and the shopworkers look as if they were dressed for *shabbos,* "the Sabbath."

The prevailing mood in the shtetl was tranquility and innocence; here tranquility has given way to bewilderment, and innocence has evolved into vigor and optimism. In the Old Country there existed a lingering feeling of hope, the traditional Jewish *bytokhen,* a hope that had its roots in mystical beliefs; in the New Country optimism was no longer mystical but rooted in reality.

Some of these photos are of such beauty that we may be inclined to look at them as pieces of art rather than as documents of human experience. But we should not give in to that feeling, for it would be a misrepresentation. The majority of American Jews—and in a deeper sense, all who have been driven from their old homes and who have felt alienated in the new—will recognize the essential truth which these photos illustrate: that under the waves of constant change, there is a basic changelessness.

The Jews of Eastern Europe came to the New Country not as adventurers or goaded by the prospect of riches. They came as victims of persecution, intolerance, misery, and police-organized pogroms. Forced to leave the land upon which they had lived for hundreds of years, they hoped to bring, together with their pots and pans and rolling pins, their graters and feather pillows, the lifestyle they had created in the Old Country. But the attempt to transplant the shtetl to American soil was not completely successful.

The Old Country tried to survive in the new environment, against opposition from without and from within the community, and it gradually was forced to submit; but while submitting it managed to retain, in altered forms, some of its basic values. It also made a lasting impact on the surrounding society, instilling some of its own ethnic qualities into the character of the adopted country.

The history of the Jews in the New World might perhaps be seen—greatly simplified—as a drama in three acts, to which could be added a romantic and half-legendary prologue. Several members of Christopher Columbus's expedition are believed to have been Spanish Jews who, under the threat of the Inquisition, had converted to Catholicism but secretly continued to practice Judaism. One was a man called Rodrigo de Triana; another was Luis de Torres. Rodrigo de Triana, who traveled aboard the *Pinta,* was the first to sight the American shore. Luis de Torres served as interpreter on the *Santa Maria,* and after Columbus landed he was sent on a diplomatic mission to seek out the great Khan of India (since Columbus believed he had arrived in India). De Torres thus was the first European on American soil, and one of the first to describe the natives.

Act I began 162 years later. In 1654 Portugal invaded the Dutch colony of Recife, off the Brazilian coast, driving out the original Dutch administration and thereby threatening the many Jews who had settled there to enjoy religious tolerance. Most of the Jews escaped back to Holland, but in the autumn of that year four men, two women, and seventeen children found themselves, after many adventures on the *Santa Katerina,* otherwise known as *St. Charles,* in the port of the tiny Dutch village of New Amsterdam, presided over by Peter Stuyvesant. Among the burghers who greeted the new arrivals was Israel Barsamson, who had arrived several weeks earlier, probably as a trader with the Dutch West India Company, which had a number of Jewish stockholders.

At first Stuyvesant was unwilling to let the Jewish refugees settle among his Christian citizens. Under pressure from the Dutch company, however, he finally agreed to let them remain, and they became the first Jewish settlement in the land that was to become the United States.

Other Sephardic Jews from Spain and Portugal began to trickle into the colonies along the Atlantic Coast. For the next two hundred years their number was negligible. In fact, at the time of the American Revolution, there were fewer than three thousand Jews in the thirteen colonies. The Sephardim had meanwhile achieved social status and become part of the American élite as executives of corporations, as directors of museums and hospitals. But due to their diminishing Jewish awareness, the growing number of intermarriages, they were in peril of disappearing as Jews.

Act II began around 1812, in the climactic years of the Napoleonic Wars, when thousands of Jews from Bavaria and Posen sought refuge in America. The collapse of the revolution of 1848 in Germany, Bohemia, Austria, and Hungary brought to the New World many more Jews, wealthier and better educated than their immediate predecessors.

They came in greater numbers than the Sephardim, and settled in larger communities. Because of their energy and enterprise they began to play an important role in American commerce and finance. Some, starting as peddlers, soon opened retail shops which later developed into department stores. Others got involved in industry and banking. Many became active in developing Jewish community life, organizing charities, hospitals, orphanages, old age homes, loan societies, and schools. Act II ended in 1871, when the immigration of German Jews came to a halt. The reason for this was the unification of Germany under Bismarck and the attendant prospects for a better life.

Although the few thousand early Sephardic Jews in the United States looked with condescension upon the 250,000 German Jews, whom they called a "nation of peddlers," deriding their heavy German accents, the German Jews had managed to establish themselves quite comfortably and peacefully. But their tranquility was disrupted by the next wave of Jewish immigration, the great surge of Jews from Eastern Europe which began Act III. In the course of thirty years more than 2.5 million Yiddish-speaking Jews—families, large groups, and in some cases entire communities—crossed the Atlantic.

That mass migration has often been called an "exodus," comparable to the biblical Exodus from Egypt. But that analogy is only partially correct.

During the exodus of the Eastern European Jews, the Russian Pharaohs were not smitten with pestilence, the Atlantic was not parted by a divine rod. There was no Moses to guide them safely. Only the bondage from which they tried to escape was similar to that of the refugees from Egypt: the inhumanity of the Czars, the misery, the pogroms organized by the police to channel peasant dissatisfaction and despair into anti-Semitism. They did not leave with "accumulated riches"; they crossed the ocean in cattle ships. The sea didn't "behold and flee," the Jordan didn't "fall back," neither did the mountains "skip like rams."

In Czarist Russia, the "Prison of Nations," Jews were at the bottom of the social ladder. Konstantin Pobyedonostzev, advisor to Alexander III (1881–94), formulated a solution for dealing with the Jewish minority: baptize one third, physically destroy one third, and force the rest to emigrate. The Russian Orthodox Church offered a long list of privileges to Jews who would submit to baptism, but very few took advantage of such offers. Anti-Jewish regulations climaxed in the infamous May Law of 1882. Pogroms started in the 1880s and increased in the 1890s. But that was merely a prelude to the massacres which took place in the years 1903–1906, when hundreds of Jewish towns were devastated; men, women, and children were killed; thousands were crippled; and a greater number were ruined economically. The "success" of that part of Pobyedonostzev's plan fulfilled the Czarist dream: Russia's Jewish subjects were forced to emigrate.

When one looks back at the great movement of the shtetl to America, one tends to see it as an upheaval of gigantic proportions. In reality the beginnings were small and hesitant. The Eastern European Jews had lived for centuries within the established framework of a social and religious community, surrounded by relatives, friends, and neighbors, often ignoring reality and nourishing mystical hopes. They were not eager to get up and leave, to abandon the living and the dead. (In some cases abandoning the dead would be even most difficult of all.) To go where? To a land which was fearfully remote, to a country of strange people and an alien tongue.

But worsening conditions were pushing them in that inevitable direction. Even without the special anti-Semitic restrictions of the Russian government, the economic crisis was becoming intolerable, and the very future of the shtetl was in doubt. The newly freed peasants were encouraged by the government to form cooperatives, which eliminated the role of the Jewish trader. The development of the railway put an end to the usefulness of Jewish cabmen and wagoners. The construction of factories ruined Jewish artisans. The introduction of monopolies on such articles as alcohol, tobacco, and salt excluded Jewish merchants. The inhabitants of the shtetl began moving to the poor, overcrowded Jewish neighborhoods in the bigger cities, swelling the number of craftsmen and petty tradesmen, causing a violent struggle for survival.

Despite the fact that in some cities Jews constituted 30, 40, and even 50 percent of the population, they were barred from all government jobs. In a city where every second inhabitant was a Jew it was unthinkable to see a Jewish postman, sanitation man, or city official of even the lowest rank.

Old values began to crumble. Jewish youths started to look for solutions outside the old social framework. Some turned to revolutionary movements, to Marxism and Socialism, to Bakunin and Kropotkin, dreaming of a new world of solidarity and brotherhood. In others the oppression evoked a longing for a Jewish state, a desire once and for all to become "a nation like other nations," to stop being "the grease on the wheels of history." But such dreams remained unattainable.

At a time of such extreme economic pressure, of growing skepticism, futile dreams, and despair, a new hope suddenly exploded in the midst of the Jewish settlements of Eastern Europe. The market places, *shuls,* "synagogues," and homes began reverberating with the magic word *America.*

The old Messiah who was to deliver the Children of Israel from their bondage had tarried too long. And the new Messiah, America, did not demand unlimited patience. The new Messiah was real, waiting at the ports of New York, of Boston, of Galveston, holding out a torch, inviting all those who were poor, tired, and yearning to be free.

At first only the bravest and most adventurous dared answer the call. Soon their letters began to arrive back home, carrying tangible proof that the new Messiah was real. The letters contained greetings from the New Land, snapshots of those who had left the shtetl as poor butcher boys or destitute little tailors and who now posed wearing "European" clothes, smart coats, hats, and even spectacles like the wealthiest householders of the shtetl, the *balebatim.* Some of the letters contained banknotes which, when translated into rubles, constituted a fortune: one could get two Russian Czars for one American President. Above all, the letters related that "over there" Jews, synagogues, and rabbis existed—in other words, the old God, who in the past had accompanied his people across borders, rivers, and seas, had now also crossed the Atlantic Ocean.

But the facts about the New Country very soon became embellished with legends. The "land of opportunity" didn't simply mean that one could make a living there. Millionaires grew like mushrooms after a rain. The road to riches stood open for anyone; all American millionaires had started out as newspaper sellers or shoeshine boys. The only thing needed was determination and will.

It all sounded believable. Everybody knew somebody who knew somebody who knew the son of a *cheder melamed,* a "primary school teacher," who had just sent his parents a letter containing a bundle of dollars and a photo in which the illiterate boy, who could hardly count up to two, was now wearing a "Prince Albert" and an aristocratic hat; from the pocket of his vest one could see the dangling chain of a gold watch. When people gathered in the *shuls,* in the market place, or in stores, the only topic of conversation was America. Letters were read aloud and reread, and each word was commented upon as though it were holy writ. America became everyone's dream.

But the dream was not altogether flawless. Along with enthusiastic letters praising the New Land came others that spoke of disappointments. American Yiddish newspapers reaching Eastern Europe described tenement houses and sweatshops. Some Yiddish songs of revolt, conceived in the slums of New York's Lower East Side, found their way to revolutionary groups in the shtetl.

Sometimes a shtetl inhabitant, a former water carrier or poor wagoner who had emigrated years earlier and become prosperous, returned on a visit, showing off his clothes, his diamond ring, and his gold watch; bestowing lavish donations for repairing the *shul* or for a new boiler in the ritual bath. He was received with great awe, thanked with gratefulness, but also with a feeling of apprehension. So this was America? Where an ignoramus, a *grober yung,* who could hardly read the "small letters," could become a success?

Others also were unexcited about America. The very pious feared with justification that in America the foundations of *Yiddishkeit* would be imperiled. The men of high social status feared—again with good reason—that in America their prestige would mean little or nothing. And many young Socialists and anarchists considered it their duty to remain on the "battle front," to fight for a better social order instead of running away. Finally, Eastern Europe, not unlike the West, had its share of assimilated Jews who believed they could, in spite of everything, become part of Russian society, culture, and spiritual life. Their number, however, was small, and eventually many of them also joined the exodus.

But letters continued to arrive and the shtetls continued to live in a state of fever. Some of the letter writers slipped in a few English words which were quickly picked up, and one could hear a woman boast that her son is no longer a *griner,* a greenhorn, that he was a "regular *Amerikaner."* The biggest event was the arrival of a steamship ticket. Such a day was a holiday, not only for the recipient but also for the whole community. The news spread quickly and the fortunate soul became an instant celebrity. Relatives, neighbors, friends, and acquaintances came to say *mazel tov,* to express their joy, to shed a few tears, and to bring their blessings. Some potential emigrants even made a pilgrimage to receive a blessing from a rabbi. Saying farewell was a long and emotional procedure, which included a visit to the cemetery to say goodbye to deceased relatives and to ask for their intervention against the perils of the voyage.

The final act of leavetaking was a procession with the participation of the whole town. It resembled both a funeral and a wedding. Everybody gave advice to the departing on how to behave on the ship in order to avoid seasickness, how to speak to the officials in New York, and how to go about becoming a millionaire.

In order to leave the country one had to possess a passport, which usually required an expensive trip to a city and exposure to hostile treatment by Russian bureaucrats. Political refugees, fleeing from Czarist gendarmes, and recruits running from military conscription, could escape only by being smuggled across the border. Tens of thousands of Jewish families, loaded with packs, baskets, and bundles, also chose this illegal method, in spite of the many dangers involved. Some fell victim to swindlers who robbed them of their possessions and abandoned them in no-man's land. But that did not stop others from following the same path.

After leaving Russia, the journey continued on over-crowded, dilapidated, filthy trains to ports of embarkation: Hamburg, Bremen, or Liverpool. Jewish committees, organized in Berlin, Paris, and London, helped the emigrants through the complicated formalities required before a ship could be boarded.

Steamship companies which had carried German Jews before the emigration from Germany had dried up, now bitterly competed for the new human cargo. Subagents of various shipping companies flooded Eastern Europe with circulars, printed in Yiddish, promising fantastic luxuries to the immigrants. But since steamship companies like White and Red Star, or the Cunard Line, could make a profit only by squeezing the maximum human cargo into a ship, the conditions under which the emigrants traveled were appalling. Squashed in steerage, they slept on mattresses filled with seaweed; each compartment was a dormitory for two or three hundred men, women, and children, who suffered from lack of ventilation, awful food, and seasickness on a voyage that lasted from eleven to seventeen days. Because of Jewish dietary laws, many passengers did not eat the food provided by the ships and lived on herring and water. Only much later did the ships provide kosher food.

But crossing the Atlantic was not a totally miserable experience. The ships were filled with people of various nationalities, mostly poor. During calmer days the ships resounded with Polish, Italian, Serbian, Russian, or Greek folk songs. Some of the Jews added their songs in Yiddish, and the religious, wrapped in black-and-white-striped prayer shawls, intoned their ancient Hebrew prayers.

Many writers have tried to describe the moment when the Jews of the shtetl, where the tallest building had been a house of one or two stories, caught their first glimpse of the New York skyline. But that wasn't the only shock. Until 1892 they had to pass through the purgatory of the "reception center" at Castle Garden, at the tip of Manhattan, which was eventually replaced by the better-organized and more spacious facility on Ellis Island. Arriving at the American shore, however, was no guarantee that one would be admitted into the New Country. The Statue of Liberty, erected in 1886 to greet the "huddled masses," often seemed to have a heart made of bronze also.

Every immigrant had to undergo a series of tests which began with a medical examination for trachoma, tuberculosis, skin diseases, and mental disorder. Not all of the immigration officers were courteous or sympathetic. After the medical examination, each immigrant received a number and was led through a battery of shrewd and often tricky questions. Who are you? What brought you here? Why did you come? The immigrant knew that his fate depended on the right answers. The danger of deportation was real; ship captains were obliged to take back any "cargo" that had been refused. A considerable number were detained or quarantined in primitive hospitals.

In March 1909, the *Jewish Daily Forward,* a Yiddish newspaper, printed the following appeal from over a hundred immigrants detained on Ellis Island:

Esteemed Mr. Editor:

Have pity on us, the unhappy people who are imprisoned on Ellis Island. Please, print our letter in your worthy paper so that our American brothers may know how we are suffering.

Most of us are Russian Jews who cannot return to Russia. We are political refugees or deserters from the army. Many of us have sold everything to have enough for the passage to America.

You know very well what a Jewish emigrant must go through before he gets to America. First of all, the difficulties with the borders; later he is put in a train like a piece of luggage on the way to the port, where he lies for many days in a shed waiting for the arrival of the ship. On the ship every emigrant is looked on like a dog. After the torment, when with the help of God he arrives in America, he must show that he is in possession of twenty-five dollars. Where is he going to get it? Who has ever heard of such a treatment of human beings? For this sort of nonsense they ruin the lives of so many people and deport them to the countries from which they have escaped.

It would be impossible to describe everything that is taking place here, on Ellis Island. We are crammed over a thousand people in a place where there is hardly place for two hundred. We are not allowed to go out for fresh air. We lie on a filthy floor. We don't have our luggage with us, and we cannot change our shirts for many weeks.

People go around in despair, everybody cries and moans. Men are kept separated from their wives and children. They can see each other only when they take us to eat. They don't let a husband talk to his wife or a father talk to his child. Many children get sick, some are taken to hospitals, some never come back.

Today is a holiday, the Fourth of July, and because of this they don't deport anybody. But tomorrow the slaughter will start again. There are some who think of jumping into the water if they will take them to the boat.

Dear Mr. Editor, our hope is that you will print this letter which was written by one of our emigrants, a student from the university of Petersburg, on the Fourth of July 1909. This is the eve of the seventeenth day of the month of Tammuz, when Jews fast in memory of the destruction of Jerusalem.

Signed: Alexander Rudnev

In 1914, 3,860 Jewish immigrants out of 130,000 were detained on Ellis Island for physical infirmities or because they were likely to become "public charges." The Jewish aid society, HIAS, and other organizations had to intervene to save those unfortunates from deportation. Of the 3,860 detained, 1,944 were admitted on bond, thanks largely to the HIAS bureau at Ellis Island.

The ships kept bringing growing numbers of Eastern European Jews. In 1881, 40,000 arrived; in 1889, 63,000 came; in 1906, the number had reached 154,000.

Many of the lucky ones who passed all examinations still had to remain in the reception center until they were claimed by relatives or potential employers. There they were fed and housed by Jewish organizations. Those with trades

—tailors, tanners, furriers, or cobblers—were often hired by entrepreneurs who waited in Battery Park for the arriving shiploads of immigrants. Also waiting were agents from boarding houses, cabbies ready to take the immigrants anywhere, thieves and con men, and some employers offering jobs in Philadelphia or places as far away as Nashville, Tennessee. Those without relatives or a profession could still be picked up by their fellow townsmen, who had organized societies to aid new arrivals from their particular shtetl.

In most cases, though, the way from Ellis Island led to the Lower East Side in New York. Newcomers were greeted with the derisive question, "Have you brought along the shovel?"—to dig up the streets allegedly paved with gold. Actually, the Land of Opportunity seemed to be composed mostly of slums, a maze of streets overshadowed by gloomy tenements and later by "dumbbell" apartment buildings: prison-like, airless brick structures with narrow doors, small windows, cramped passages, and dangerously steep staircases. Apartments in such buildings usually consisted of a living room and kitchen, with between them a windowless and doorless alcove which served as the bedroom.

Entire streets were turned into markets, crammed with hundreds of pushcarts. Amid deafening noise, peddlers called out their wares: damaged eggs, candles, hats, dried fruit, herring, sausages, pins and needles, buttons, *potatoniks,* chicken legs, chicken wings, or eyeglasses which served not to improve the customer's vision but, for the price of a quarter, to make him look like a doctor. The Lower East Side had few saloons; "having a drink" meant having a glass of seltzer or soda water with grape juice.

Since families were rarely in a position to afford the full rent charged them, they took in lodgers, and sometimes the fire escape landing became an additional bedroom. Until 1901, there was no building code with minimum standards for toilets, running water, fire escapes, staircases, or the size of windows. But even after the introduction of a code, apartments remained dark, damp, and tiny. In the daytime, the living room served as a shop where the family, including all the children, and often the lodgers, were busy making cigars, sewing, or mending.

If living conditions were harsh, working conditions were even worse. A popular song of the Yiddish theater which had managed to reach the shtetl—"Long Live Columbus"—now had ironic connotations.

In the early 1880s most of the immigrants had no professions at all. They were qualified only for unskilled and wretchedly paid work. But even those with professions worked fourteen hours a day, eighty-four hours a week. Needleworkers had to provide their own sewing machines, which they carried on their shoulders while walking up and down flights of stairs looking for work.

Despite appalling living and working conditions, disease was less widespread in the Jewish slum sections than in the non-Jewish neighborhoods. The reason for this was the strictly observed dietary laws, while the lack of hygienic facilities in the tenements was overcome by the establishment of public baths.

The newcomer soon discovered that the exchange of the Old Country for the New meant more than a change of scenery, of living conditions, or of work habits. The transition went deeper. The immigrant was in for a series of radical shocks.

It started with a revolution of time. For over six hundred years the Jews of Eastern Europe had lived with a peculiar time concept: time in the shtetl had a past and a future but no present. The inhabitants of the shtetl were intimately acquainted with biblical events; the characters of the Bible were not fictitious or legendary. They seemed almost contemporary, like relatives, neighbors who lived across the street or even in the same house, patriarchs, kings, judges, prophets. It was even possible to imagine that God himself would occasionally descend from his Seventh Heaven to sit in the shtetl's *beth midrash,* "house of study," or hide behind the embroidered curtain of the holy ark, listening to the congregations's prayers. Even obscure characters of the Bible or ancient Jewish history, such as Arpachshad, Meshach, or the Emperor Titus, were more familiar than Bismarck, Wellington, or the ministers of the Czar.

The shtetl lived in close relationship with the past, in a state of waiting for the future: the coming of the Messiah. The Messiah was real, his coming was certain. There were

Jews who slept with their clothes near their bed, ready at any moment to arise at the blowing of the ram's horn, which would be the signal to get up and follow him to the city of Jerusalem.

The present was ignored. Of course one had to live, and living forced one to look for a livelihood and often gave rise to human weaknesses, for the spirit of the Devil was always about. But all that was accepted as secondary. The six week days were merely a preparation for the holy day of *shabbos,* and *shabbos* was the foretaste of things to come.

The first and perhaps most powerful shock for the Eastern European Jews who came to America was a revolution of time: the emergence of the present. It was easy to imagine the patriarch Abraham or the prophet Jeremiah walking through the shtetl, sitting on the stairs of the ritual bath. It was no longer easy to imagine their presence on Ludlow Street in New York or on Chestnut Street in Philadelphia. In the New Country, the past melted into the remote layers of consciousness; the future was no longer wrapped in mysticism. Life in the New Country was no longer an act of waiting; it was a life to be lived. That demanded a complete change in daily practices and an evolution of values.

Religion in the shtetl was a discipline that occupied all twenty-four hours of the day. In the New Country the tempo of life made it impossible to devote all one's time to God. Everything was shortened: the time for serving God, the beard, the length of the coat. Old *tzitzis* (the fringed garments biblical law insisted be worn by every male) were not replaced. Only the very pious now used their prayer shawls every day.

Shabbos itself lost its sacredness. It was no more the "foretaste of things to come." In the shtetl, holidays and *shabbos* had been distinguished by special prayers and a different sort of behavior, rituals, and food. Black bread was for the six days of the week; on the day of the Sabbath the table was adorned with a loaf of *challah,* white *shabbos* bread. Here one could eat white bread in the middle of the week. Similarly, special holiday foods—cheese blintzes for *Shevuoth, matzoth* for Passover, *hamantashen* (three-cornered pastries stuffed with poppy seeds) for Purim, and *latkes* (potato pancakes) for Chanukah—could be obtained from the grocer all year round. Gone was the solemnity of preparing the food, gone was the mother's elaborate regular ceremony of making noodles; ready-made noodles could be bought in cardboard boxes.

In the shtetl one was very rarely exposed to contact with the non-Jewish world. Such contacts were brief and remained on the level of commercial dealing, and it was usually the women who provided for the family, who dealt with the non-Jew. The husband's communication was limited to his family, neighbors, and congregation in the *shul.* This made it unnecessary to learn another language; he spoke Yiddish to his fellows and Hebrew to God.

In the New Country those conditions were no longer the

same. Even when newcomers did try to recreate the shtetl on the Lower East Side, the impact of the city made sharp demands on them. The immigrant no longer could—or even wanted to—ignore the non-Jewish society. The sudden, tangible contact with the outside world had a revolutionary impact on all aspects of his life, material as well as spiritual, extending even to the world of the dead.

In the Old Country separation from the world of the non-Jew persisted with even greater strictness after death. Jewish dead were buried in exclusively Jewish cemeteries. A cemetery was a holy place, and it would be inconceivable for a deceased Jew to have a non-Jewish neighbor. Not so in the New Country. American Yiddish literature offers many stories describing funerals where the mourners, following the casket, suddenly realize they are walking through rows of tombstones marked with crosses. At first this was a traumatic experience, but it was a fact of life to be accepted.

Another shock to greet the newcomer was the breakdown of the social structure, which in the shtetl had been based on the division between wealthy and poor, learned and humble. The shtetl had a name for these two groups—*shayne yiden* and *proste yiden,* "beautiful Jews" and "simple Jews." Respect was given to some not for personal merit but because of dignity they had inherited from their ancestors. Those who received that respect disdained physical work.

In America the evaluation of an individual was based no longer on the position he had enjoyed in the Old Country, but on his own personal achievement. The question was no longer "Who *were* you?" but rather that characteristic American phrase, "Who do you think you are?"—*you,* and not your great-grandfather.

The gap between *shayne yiden* and "simple Jews" disappeared. Physical work was not frowned upon. The New Country maintained a cult of work, personal exertion, and personal achievement. Work was not something to be ashamed of, but a matter of pride and dignity.

The *shayner yid* of yesterday was put in a sweatshop together with a fellow townsman who "over there" might have been a simple butcher or water carrier. No French Revolution could have performed that miracle of egalitarianism with more thoroughness.

When the *shayner yid* came to his *landsmanshaft* (a society of people from the same shtetl), he might find that the president of the society was the man who had been the shtetl's cobbler or water carrier. A new word entered the vocabulary—"success," which could only come as the result of personal initiative and ingenuity. The French aristocrat Alexis de Tocqueville, who visited New York in 1831, was impressed "by the spirit of equality that pervaded the life and the customs of the people . . . a commitment to equality which was in striking contrast to the class-ridden society of Europe."

The revolution in social hierarchy was no less radical in its effect on the family structure, which had existed uninterrupted for many centuries. The family cell, with its ruling husband, submissive wife, and obedient children, began to disintegrate. The new reality equalized the position of husband and wife. Children began to work very early, including the girls. The fact that children could pick up the new language much more quickly than their parents gave them an unprecedented importance in the family. They almost instantly became Americanized, while the parents remained greenhorns for many years, if not for the rest of their lives. This was a blow to the long-established patriarchy. The father not only lost his position of unquestioned respect, he also became the object of his children's embarrassment. A new saying was added to the immigrant's folklore: "America? This is a country where the children educate their parents." Early Jewish-American literature is full of accounts of the crumbling of the father's position and the traumatic discomfort of his children. The blessing of the new equality was accompanied by side effects with which it was hard to cope.

America was a free country. Opportunities were equal for everyone. A Jew could even become a policeman! For a man who had lived under the perennial fear of the Czarist gendarmes, with the power of life and death in their hands, policemen who were Jewish truly signified the existence of the Messiah.

For the first time in a long history, Jews from Eastern Europe came to a land of tolerance and freedom; the U.S.

Constitution clearly stated that all men were created equal. Poland, too, had had a constitution with a similar clause, but over there it had been an empty phrase; here it was practiced in real life. No wonder the immigrant repaid that tolerance with instant loyalty. Only a few days after his arrival in this country, the immigrant felt he belonged. A Russian Jew would never, even after centuries, say about himself that he was a Russian. Neither would a Jew in Lithuania say he was a Lithuanian. In America the immigrant immediately became a partner of other immigrants gathered from all parts of the world.

But that new freedom and equality were also a source of anxiety. In Eastern Europe freedom was restricted by laws and anti-Jewish decrees. Other restrictions existed within the Jewish community itself. One had to tread cautiously on a narrow path which made life hard, but which also was a route safely charted out in advance. In the New Country the onslaught of freedom—and it was a genuine onslaught—was so overwhelming that it confused values. When direct responsibility before God or community disappeared, the immigrant found himself in a state of anarchy, exposed to a multitude of contradicting ideas; he had to find answers to unaccustomed questions, answers which no book on his shelf provided. Apart from the confusing freedom, the new reality introduced a new concept: material success, respect for material values, for the dollar. People were evaluated according to their income. Everything could be bought and sold. Tickets were sold not only to the theater but to the synagogue for the services of the High Holy Days.

The division between sacred and profane was wiped out. Cantors were famous not only for their voices, but for the size of their salaries. Many cantors performed as actors on the stage, or prepared themselves to sing in the opera or in Broadway musicals. Synagogue executives used gimmicks to draw in "customers." Bar mitzvahs and weddings, holy occasions in the Old Country, were turned into performances. Even funerals became part of an industry. Old concepts of morality began to crumble. Free love and uninhibited sex were considered symbols of Americanization.

The religious saw danger to religion; the Socialist, who had imported from the Old Country strict faithfulness to the theories of his teachers, saw in the New Country an abandonment of principle, a reigning spirit of selfishness and hyprocrisy. Both the religious and the secular found themselves in a similar state of confusion. However, there was one consolation: the children.

As God had said to Abraham, "Unto thy seed will I give this land." America may have been a bitter experience for the parents, but it was easier to endure with the knowledge that life was not a blind alley, as it had been in the shtetl. For the children there was an opportunity for education. High schools and universities freely accepted the sons and daughters of the poor as well as the rich. The Old Country hope that one's children might escape from the trap of misery became a reality. According to a popular anecdote, a Jewish mother, when asked about the age of her two children, replied, "The doctor is two and the lawyer is three."

The first Yiddish newspapers and periodicals in the New Country appeared in the late 1880s. Most of them were modeled after German papers. The *Jewish Daily Forward,* whose lifelong editor, Abraham Cahan, was an immigrant from Lithuania, gained the greatest popularity. When Cahan took over the reins of the daily, he had already established himself in English as a writer of fiction. A Socialist of the Russian school, he had very early caught the spirit of the New Country, in which the rigid sectarianism imported from Europe was an anachronism. He knew at first hand that the primary concern of Yiddish immigrants was not the "breaking of chains," "the overthrow of tyrants," but the daily human problems of survival.

Cahan considered himself more than simply an editor and supplier of news. His aim was to make the *Forward* a guide, a popular university, which could actively help its readers, mostly greenhorns, cope with the obstacles of an immigrant's life. He introduced many journalistic novelties. He published articles about American manners and etiquette, wrote about the highlights of American history, and explained the intricacies of baseball.

Above all, he encouraged his readers to look to the *Forward* for advice. He created the column *A Bintel Brief,*

"A Bundle of Letters," which from its inception became the most popular feature in the newspaper. A great dialogue commenced; readers flooded the *Forward* with letters to the "esteemed editor," in which they opened their hearts, presented their problems; and Cahan, the oracle, tried to answer them. Those letters, preserved in the archives of the *Forward,* have been gathered into an anthology, *A Bintel Brief,* New York: Doubleday, 1971, edited by one of the prominent *Forward* writers, Isaac Metzker. Here are some of these letters, in a very condensed form, together with the paraphrased reply of the "oracle."

I am a greenhorn. I came five weeks ago from Russia where I left a blind father and a stepmother. When I arrived in New York I walked around for two weeks looking for a job; in the third week I found a job, at which I earn eight dollars a week. I paid my landlady, bought a few pieces of clothing, and I still have a few dollars in my pocket. Now I want you to tell me what to do. Should I send my father a few dollars for Passover, or should I keep the small amount of money for myself?

Answer: Send a few dollars; it is easier for you to earn a living in New York than for a blind father in Russia.

I worked for a long time in a shop with a Gentile girl. We began to go out together and we fell in love. We decided to get married and we agreed that I would remain a Jew and she a Christian. But a year after our marriage I began to notice that she is being drawn back to her Christian religion. She gets up on Sundays, runs to the church, and comes back with eyes swollen from crying. What should we do?

Answer: Mixed marriages mostly end in tragedies. Move to a Jewish neighborhood, where a husband might have more influence over his wife.

I am a working man from Bialystok, where I belonged to the Jewish Socialist party, the Bund. Here, in New York, I work in a jewelry store and earn good wages. But my heart cannot remain silent over the blood of my brethren which is spilled in Russia. Should I fulfill my duty to my parents and bring them to America, or go back to Russia and help my comrades in their struggle?

Answer: Bring the parents to this country and be useful here in local social movements.

I am a Russian revolutionist and an atheist. Here in America I met a girl who is also a freethinker. We decided to marry, but her Orthodox parents demand that we should have a religious ceremony. How should we act?

Answer: It pays to give in to old parents and not cause them any worries. Later you can go on living as freethinkers.

I am a young man of twenty and I have a seventeen-year-old cousin. I like the girl; she is American-born, well-educated, and not bad-looking. But she is very small, while I happen to be tall. When we walk down the street people stare at us and call us names. They call me *loksh*, "macaroni" and her they call *blintze.* I ask you, dear editor, could this lead to a difficult life if we decided to get married?

Answer: It is better for the man to be taller and the woman shorter. Had it been the other way around, then it would have presented a problem. As for the people who stare—let them stare.

I am a girl from Galicia. In the shop where I work, I sit close to a Jew from Russia. He keeps insulting all the Galician Jews. He says that they are all no good, he wishes all the Galician Jews to be dead. Esteemed editor, does he have a right to say such things?

Answer: There are good Galician Jews and there are bad. You are a good one. There are good Russian Jews and there are bad ones. He is not only bad; he also is an idiot.

My parents have five children. I am the oldest, a girl of fourteen. We have been in the country two years, and my father is the only one who works and supports the whole family. I go to school, where I do well, but I think of giving up my learning and helping Father. My parents don't want to hear about it. They want me to continue with my studies. I beg you to advise me what to do.

Answer: Obey your parents and continue with your education; this will give them greater satisfaction.

I am a married woman with two little children. I am a very good wife; I don't neglect the house or my family. But although I am a woman I want to be educated. I started to go twice a week to evening classes. My husband is not happy about this. Please tell me, what is your opinion?

Answer: As long as a wife does not neglect her family, she has the right to go to school two evenings a week. She has the same right to be educated as the man has.

A long, sad year has gone by since I left home. I am not happy. My homesickness and loneliness make my life bitter. Home, beloved home! My heart goes out to my parents whom I left behind. I want to run home. I entreat you to advise me how to act.

Answer: All immigrants are like plants that are transplanted to new soil. At first they wither, but in time they revive and take root in the new ground.

I am a woman of seventy and I write this letter with the blood of my heart. In the Old Country, in Galicia, my husband was a respected businessman. God gave us three sons and two daughters. When they grew up they left the nest like birds and went to America. Only our oldest son stayed, and got married, but a month later he went swimming and drowned. After this tragedy my husband became sick and died. I longed for the children, who brought me over to America. But here a new trouble has fallen on me. Austria has declared war on Russia, and my two sons, who are patriots of the Kaiser Franz Josef, want to go home and help him in the war. I am terribly distressed. What should I tell them?"

Answer: Thank God they live in America, where they are free and nobody can force them to shed their blood for an Austrian Kaiser.

I am from a small town in Russia. My father died when I was a child. A pogrom broke out and my mother was one of the first victims of the murderers. But that wasn't enough for them; they also robbed me of my honor. I begged them to kill me, but they wouldn't listen and left me to suffer. Later my relatives brought me over to America. Here I met a young and decent man and we fell in love. He wants to marry me and is waiting for my answer. I want to become his wife but I keep putting it off, for I cannot tell him the grave secret. What should I do?

Answer: In the pogroms many Jewish girls suffered that misfortune. Don't feel guilty, because you are innocent. If the young man is honest and decent, he will be able to understand.

When the Children of Israel entered the Promised Land, the only people they encountered were the native Canaanites. Things were different when the shtetl came to the shores of America. Here, the Eastern European immigrants were met by German Jews who had settled earlier, and the meeting was not a happy one. The German Jews were appalled by the scrawny little men with their beards and sidelocks, the ancient-looking women with scarfs around their wigs, behaving noisily, gesticulating, and talking Yiddish, that "monstrous and abominable garbled slang," which was a "violated" German.

The first encounter between the two groups had actually occurred earlier, when many of the immigrants, on their way to the embarkation ports, had stopped in Berlin. The German Jews, with that old urge to practice charity, had felt responsibility to provide help, but at the same time they were reluctant to organize aid committees, fearing that that might only encourage more Russian Jews to leave the Pale and arrive in even greater numbers. When the first emigrants arrived at the Charlottenburg railway station in Berlin, they caused such a stir of curiosity among the local population and the press that the *Yahudim* (as the Eastern European Jews called the German Jews derisively) could not ignore their existence. Hurriedly they organized committees to provide food, shelter and, most of all, passage money to speed the Eastern European Jews as quickly as possible to America.

When the two groups met again, in America, the second

encounter was even more traumatic because this time there would be no moving on. Most of the German Jews, who then lived in lower and mid-Manhattan and in other communities across the country, had become prosperous and gained prestige among their non-Jewish neighbors. After the disaster of the 1848 revolution in Germany, where they had tried to be more German than the Germans, they had been ungratefully repaid with anti-Semitism. Emigrating from the beloved *Vaterland* was bitter, but the New Country offered some consolation. As before, in Germany, the German Jews wanted to be flawless citizens. But they always retained a deep apprehension that something might happen to disturb their tranquility and bring back the shadows of a traumatic past.

With the arrival of the first ships carrying the new human cargo from the East, those fears seemed to materialize. Some of the shocked German Jews, viewing those "Orientals," that "medieval rubbish," immediately voiced the old Jewish concern: "What will the *goyim* say?"

"Their continued residence among us may result in a lowering of the opinion in which the American Jews are held," said the secretary of the Hebrew Emigrant Aid Society.

"It would be wise to send missionaries to Russia to civilize them, otherwise they will Russianize us," said the *Jewish Messenger.*

"We cannot afford to permit the influx of these oppressed Russians to become the standard upon which we shall be judged," said the *American Israelite.*

Yahudim-led organizations sent telegrams to Europe: "Send no more. We must return incapables," or "We shall not be a party to the infliction upon our community of a class of migrants whose only destiny is the hospital, the infirmary, or the workhouse."

"If you send more Russians to Milwaukee," telegraphed a German Jew to a Jewish organization in New York, "they will be shipped back to you without permitting them to leave the depot." Those were indeed strange words of welcome for the "huddled masses yearning to be free," coming, as it were, from their own brethren.

But the invasion by the shtetl Jews continued. Most of them went no farther than New York, settling on the Lower East Side of Manhattan. Since there was no way of halting the flood, or of deporting the "Russians" (though some attempts were made), the German-Jewish aid committees decided to make the immigrants a little less visible, at least, to divert them from New York.

The Industrial Removal Office was formed to disperse some of the Jewish immigrants throughout the United States. But the results were negligible: during the eleven years of its existence, only twelve thousand newcomers were scattered over the forty-eight states and into 1,670 localities as a result of its work. Many existing communities, influenced by the committees' own propaganda, were unwilling to accept immigrants.

In 1909, another project came into being, the so-called Galveston Plan. Instead of bringing immigrant ships to New York, they would be redirected to the port of Galveston,

Texas; from there the immigrants would be dispersed over the rest of the country. But that plan also failed, since most of the new arrivals, lost and lonely, wanted to be near existing centers of Yiddish culture.

The *Yahudim* argued that the "influx of uncivilized Russians," their deteriorated tenements and unattractive pushcarts, would cause a wave of anti-Semitism. The same alarm had been expressed earlier, by the established Sephardic Jews, when the Jewish immigrants from Germany, those "peddlers and upstarts," began to arrive in America. They would, the Sephardic Jews claimed, make all Jews "stand out" in the general pattern of American life.

Now, the German Jews feared the Russian Jews would endanger their achieved positions. Yet their own position in American society was not without blemishes. In many parts of the country the German Jews themselves were excluded from Anglo-Saxon clubs; hotels displayed signs saying, "No Jews Admitted," and certain residential areas were closed to them, even though none of them wore a caftan or a beard, or spoke an "abominable Yiddish slang."

The majority of non-Jewish Americans obviously were not hostile to the arriving immigrants; Christian leaders, intellectuals, and politicians often expressed a moving compassion and offered assistance to the uprooted newcomers. There were, however, also those who called for a stop to immigration and who finally succeeded in introducing an act establishing discriminatory national and racial quotas. But that had little to do with the actual appearance or behavior of the immigrants; it mostly reflected the minds of the legislators. "The idea behind this discriminatory policy," said President Truman when he vetoed the Immigrants and Nationality Act, "is, to put it boldly, that Americans with English or Irish names are better than Americans with Italian or Greek or Polish names. Such a concept is utterly unworthy of our traditions and our ideals."

Fear of the shtetl Jews, however, was balanced by a feeling of compassion. As time went on, German Jews initiated many aid societies in New York, Charleston, Cincinnati, Chicago, St. Louis, and Philadelphia. But behind such philanthrophy also lurked an ulterior motive: to convert the "poor brethren" into "civilized" human beings. The Educational Alliance in New York, for instance, openly formulated its aim of secularizing Jewish immigrants: trim or shave their beards, remove the married women's wigs, teach immigrants to discard their jargon, and turn them into what the German Jews themselves were—American Israelites.

But in their attempts to assist and civilize the immigrants, the *Yahudim* did not take into account the recipients of their philanthrophy. The immigrants were in need of help, but they were also *proud* beggars. They would accept charity, for all of Jewish history was permeated with helping the needy. But they would never let themselves be patronized.

It was not the immigrants' stubbornness but their benefactors' ignorance which led to continuous, and often acrimonious, conflicts. The German Jews did not understand the meaning of the shtetl or the essence of Eastern European Jewish life.

Unlike the Jews of Berlin, Paris, and London, the Eastern European Jews had never tried to conceal any part of their Jewishness. They made no attempts to reform others and did not see why others should want to reform them. They believed that their way of life was right and saw no reason for abandoning it.

After all, Eastern European Jewish culture was based on the tenets of a Book which was accepted by the rest of the world. The shtetl Jew was not ashamed of his clothing, his language, the food he ate, his customs and traditions. The open display of his identity kept him free of the complexes which so painfully plagued those who tried to hide their identities, which led them to self-hatred, a disease unknown among the Jews of the shtetl. Make fun of oneself? Of course. But hate oneself? For what reason?

America, they had been told, was a country of immigrants, a haven for those who suffered because of their "different" beliefs; America was a land of political, cultural, and religious freedom—not a basic training camp for "accepted" behavior. There was no reason why they, who had arrived with a rich Jewish heritage, should submit to those who made a habit of renouncing customs and heritage.

But with the passage of time many of the immigrants

overcame their poverty by hard work, diligence, and perseverance. They were no longer in need of relief, and when assistance was necessary they organized their own philanthropic institutions. Soon the German Jews discovered an interest in the shtetl, and found delight in Yiddish jokes, Yiddish folk songs, and chopped liver. Reform temples began to invite speakers to lecture on the Old Country. Many children of German Jews began to read Sholem Aleichem and Peretz in the original. And the portraits of Eastern Europeans, of Zionists and Socialists, today adorn the living rooms of those whose parents once cabled to the immigration headquarters in Paris, "Send us no more."

In the early 1880s certain groups of young Jewish people, dressed in Russian tunics and clutching unfurled flags emblazoned with embroidered plows, began arriving in the New Country. Unlike the other immigrants, who viewed the New York skyline with awe and amazement, those young men and women virtually ignored it. They knew what they had come for: to become farmers, to build agricultural settlements according to the teachings of the ancient prophets and of Jean-Jacques Rousseau and Leo Tolstoy.

They called themselves *Am Olam*, "The Eternal People." That movement of Jewish youths had started in the 1870s in Kiev and Odessa. Its goal had been to go to America to "harvest our own bread."

Another purpose of the movement had been to show

the world that the age-old accusation of anti-Semites that Jews were inherently nothing but peddlers and moneylenders, tailors and watchmakers, was not true, that Jews had actually been forced into these trades by governments which had deprived them of the right to work the land.

They had read the works of Emerson, Thoreau, and the American transcendentalists. They planned to settle unpopulated American territories, to establish cooperative farms, where they would live in communal brotherhood, where they would combine manual labor with intellectual activities: discussing socialism and anarchism, debating the merits of vegetarianism, analyzing the teachings of Marx and Kropotkin.

The Jewish immigration organizations received them with great enthusiasm. This was what the charity people had been hoping for: Jewish immigrants who would not increase the number of pushcarts on the Lower East Side. The young idealists were promised not only land, housing, plowshares, and cattle, but also libraries and even pianos. There they would be able to combine "plain living and high thinking." Religious Jewish immigrants who expressed the wish to live on the land were promised, in addition to the implements necessary to farming, synagogues, religious primary schools, and ritual baths.

To those in the congested shtetls of the Old Country who desired to become farmers, the open prairies promised an opportunity to live in peace, liberty, and lyrical innocence. Self-sustaining farms were hurriedly organized in

Michigan, Wisconsin, Kansas, Louisiana, Oklahoma, and New Jersey.

Alas, the eagerness of those who wanted to help and the romanticism and naïveté of the would-be farmers ended, in almost all cases, in disaster. In retrospect those attempts to "show the world" have all the elements of a Chaplinesque farce.

Most committees, in their haste and ignorance, had chosen the wrong kind of land for settlements: arid, swampy, exposed to destructive elements. "Sicily Island" in Louisiana, for instance, was ruined by floods, invaded by malaria-carrying mosquitoes, plagued by poisonous snakes. Another colony, "Cremieux," in South Dakota, was built on land without sufficient water; it was destroyed several times by fire, smashed by hailstorms, ruined by drought.

The settlement in Oregon, established in 1882 and nostalgically called "New Odessa," had a flag inscribed with a quotation by Reb Hillel, "If I am not for myself, who will be?" It was ruined not by the hostility of nature, but by personal conflicts. Here the settlers had divided each day into segments, devoted to work behind the plow, to mathematics and English lessons, and to debates on intellectual subjects. But it soon became apparent that being a shepherd was beautiful in theory only and that harvesting crops was not stimulating enough for the intellect. Continuous discussions created irritations which finally led to the dissolution of the settlement for "theoretical reasons."

The endless bickering between the German-Jewish organizations and the colonists did not help either, and many colonists simply abandoned their shacks, sold their livestock and implements, and hurried to the nearest cities, where they became the opposite of what their benefactors had wanted them to be: peddlers and small businessmen.

At one time hundreds of Jewish families settled in the beautiful regions of the Catskill Mountains in New York State. After a brief stint in the fields, they found that taking in boarders for the summer was a less risky way of making a living. Strangely, that was called "summer boarder agriculture." Many of today's resorts and guest houses in the Borscht Belt owe their origin to the agricultural movement.

The only colony that prevailed, for almost a century, was the "Alliance" (named by Emma Lazarus), organized in 1882, in the vicinity of Vineland, New Jersey. It ceased to exist in 1969 after the death of its last member. There was no new generation to take over. The farmers' children, after attending high school in Vineland, failed to return to their parents' farms; they went on to college. Instead of another generation of farmers, the colony produced a crop of doctors, lawyers, and judges.

When the Am Olam movement first emerged in Kiev and Odessa, other Jewish youths, again mostly students, were obsessed by similar ideas of getting "back to nature." But they combined the idea of farming with the concept of a national Jewish state. While the members of Am Olam were organizing farms in Missouri and Oklahoma, members of Bilu (an acronym formed from the initials of *Beth*

Yaakov Lekhu Veneylekhu, "House of Jacob, let us get up and go") were building kibbutzim and cooperative agricultural or workers' settlements in Palestine. They, too, were confronted by deserts and swamps; they, too, suffered from malaria, droughts, and snakes. But those settlements prevailed, perhaps because the Tolstoyan idea of "making one's own bread" was joined with the Herzlian vision of a Jewish national home.

When the first immigrants began to arrive in New York, Yiddish in Eastern Europe was reaching the peak of its seven-hundred-year history as a language. Yiddish literature, which had begun in Western Europe during the Renaissance, influenced by wandering German folksingers and later by Italian poets, had finally become part of modern European literature in the middle of the nineteenth century.

Yiddish writing reached maturity at almost the same time as the national literature of the hosts among whom it developed and thrived—the Slavs. Modern Russian literature was born at the end of the eighteenth century. The "grandfather" of modern Yiddish literature, Mendele Mokher Sforim, was born in 1836. But even he had been preceded by others. The Jewish immigrants who arrived at the turn of this century spoke not a "jargon," but a rich language which had given birth to novels, stories, poetry, and plays.

New York, which was soon to become the largest Jewish city in all of Jewish history, thus also became an important, and eventually a leading, Jewish cultural center. At first Yiddish literature was imported from the Old Country. But very soon New York began to develop its own writers, poets, and playwrights. Some of them had come to America with reputations already established: Sholem Asch, Joseph Opatoshu, Zalmen Schneyur, H. Leivick. And one of the three founding fathers of modern Yiddish literature, Sholem Aleichem, spent his last years in New York, and died in the Bronx.

Yiddish writing in America initially shared the emotions of its readers, a nostalgia for the shtetl, where life had been *echt,* "genuine." Here it was uprooted, in flux. But soon American scenery was introduced, along with elements of "Americanism." Several young poets from Russia, filled with the teachings of Marx and Bakunin—men who had been prevented from expressing their social outrage in the Old Country by threats of prison and exile—suddenly discovered in America the horrors of a sixteen-hour working day, of sweatshops "worse than Egyptian slavery." Their wrathful poems called upon the "masses" to "break the chains," to destroy the "tyrants," to overthrow the "despots," to "sap the foundations of the satraps." The "tyrants" and the "despots" were the owners of small shops, who were hardly any wealthier than their "slaves."

"Look at him," one of the poets fumed, "look at that obese vampire of human blood, who locks his brethren in chains in order to ride on their backs." The language used in that early stage of Yiddish poetry brimmed over with exaggerated scorn. "When I see how your ruler is drinking your blood, my heart is aflame with hellish fire."

This overemotional writing was soon followed—in poetry as well as in prose—by a turn to deeper problems, describing the struggle of the immigrant for a new identity, his tortuous path of adaptation. With young and powerful voices rising in poetry and prose, the literature of the New Country slowly reached maturity. Before the first quarter of this century had passed, Yiddish culture was centered in three cities: Warsaw, Moscow, and New York. Within a few years, after the destruction of Jewish Moscow by the Bolsheviks and of Warsaw by the Nazis, New York was the only one left.

New York very quickly also became a spawning ground for the Yiddish theater, especially along Second Avenue in Manhattan. Soon there were five, eight and, at the peak, twelve Yiddish theaters. They spread to Brooklyn, the Bronx, and many other American cities.

For most of the immigrants, the Yiddish theater was not just a matter of amusement—it was a fulfillment of their cultural needs. The immigrant wanted to become an *Amerikaner* without giving up his tradition or his language. The theater greeted him with a paean to the Statue of Liberty, gave him comedies and dramas about the joys and miseries of immigrant life and, at the same time, allowed him to be nostalgic about the Old Country. Here, the audience could take revenge on traditional Jewish enemies: the Czar, the Cossacks, and the pogromchiks. The theater, with its primitive absurdities, helped the newcomer to get through the period of being a greenhorn—it taught him to be an American.

The repertoire offered was not of a very high quality. In fact, most of the plays were *shund,* a word in the vocabulary of the theater which connoted a vulgar commercialism. But then to write plays for theaters which changed programs every few days was not an easy task. Indeed, it was not a question of art so much as one of manufacturing.

Playwrights concocted plays by stealing from themselves or from other writers. They pinched plots from old operas, and "translated, adapted, and improved" the plays of Shakespeare. There was a *Jewish King Lear,* and a *Jewish Hamlet* in which Hamlet was a yeshiva student whose uncle, a rabbi, informed on his own brother and had him exiled to Siberia so he could seduce Hamlet's mother. Very often a Yiddish playwright went to the American theater to appropriate comedies and dramas, and often he did not know that what he was stealing had already been taken over from Ibsen or Strindberg.

For a long time the Yiddish theater was ruled by its stars—by the Mogulescos, the Boris Tomashevskis, the Bertha Kalishes, the David Kesslers. The star was the absolute monarch; he dictated to the writer what to write and told the director how to direct. The other actors served only one purpose: to give the star cues for his grand scenes.

To the audience the star was divine. Each one had his devoted followers, like the Hasidim in the shtetl who were totally devoted to their rebbes. The stars behaved like maharajahs. Boris Tomashevski had his own limousine, his own French chauffeur, and a Japanese valet.

A very important role was played by the prompter. He was often the only member of the cast who could read and write. He not only prompted the words; from his hole in the stage, he often instructed the actors how to move, when to cry, when to laugh, and when to giggle. He sometimes spoke louder than the actors.

The producers of those theaters often went to Europe to hire new actors and new material, or to import entire productions. Since most of the actors came from different parts of Eastern Europe, it often happened that members of a stage "family" would speak in different dialects. The father might say *ikh,* the mother *ekh,* the son *yekh,* and the daughter *yakh*—all meaning "I."

The audience, mostly sweatshop workers and peddlers, came to the theater not only to watch the play but to socialize: to meet *landsleit* and to discuss politics. It was customary to bring along one's supper and to eat it during the show. Hawkers walked down the aisles selling blintzes, knishes, and bottles of seltzer. Matchmakers used the theater by giving one ticket to a young man, and a ticket for the adjoining seat to a young woman. If he liked her, he bought her a bag of peanuts and they walked out together.

The audience reacted with great affection to the plot, crying with the wronged orphan, laughing with the comedian, applauding the idealist, scoffing at the cynic, and hating the evil-doer. Very often the villain had to leave by a back door to avoid being beaten up by a crowd ready to avenge the young orphan. At the end of the play the audience would applaud wildly and demand the appearance of the author. That happened even when the play was *Othello.*

Some of the stage effects were fantastic. When the play demanded rain, there was real water. In plays set on a farm, live goats, chickens, and even a live horse appeared on stage. When the star was on stage, the lights were bright; when he left, half the lights were turned off. To emphasize a tragic scene, the lights were extinguished. Like the commedia dell' Arte, the Yiddish theater had its singularly costumed stock characters. The hero always wore a mustache and sideburns; the villain was redheaded; a Hasid carried a colored handkerchief; a matchmaker carried an umbrella; a sexton carried a snuff box; a promoter carried a walking stick; a doctor wore glasses; a capitalist smoked a cigar; a peddler wore tattered pants; a student carried a book.

The audience frequently demanded that the star repeat a monologue, a song, or even a death scene.

Some plays were written collectively by the actors. If one of them contributed a dirge about the destruction of the Temple and the other a Chinese song, the first act would take place in Jerusalem and the second act would take place in Peking. Stage events did not always take place consistently; Abraham made a bigger impression if he smoked a cigar; King David's palace would be lit by electric chandeliers.

The history of the Yiddish theater was a continuous fight against *shund,* a struggle for the education of the public as well as the actors. One of the pioneers of the "better" theater was a gifted playwright and idealist, Jacob Gordin. He was the first to get rid of stock characters, the first to write dramas about real people. He took upon himself the task of reeducating the actors, teaching them respect for the text and respect for the audience. He taught them to stop reciting and start talking, even whispering. He purified the theatrical language. He induced the audience, which had become used to canned spectacles, to sit and watch a real human drama. He even brought the Jewish intelligentsia, which had stayed away from the cheap shows, into the theater. He wrote some forty one-act plays and dramas, including adaptations of plays by Goethe, Schiller, Hauptmann, and Gorki. His influence helped to create serious art theater and important drama clubs, such as the *Artef,* or the *Folksbiene* which exists to this day.

New important playwrights began enriching the repertoire: Peretz Hirshbein, David Pinsky, H. Leivick. And the Yiddish language grew with every play.

Some Yiddish actors, like Joseph Schildkraut, Bertha Kalish, David Kessler, and Paul Muni, were "abducted" by the English-language theater on Broadway. Strange "marriages" took place between the English and the Yiddish theater, as when the great star of Second Avenue, Jacob Adler, played in *The Merchant of Venice* on Broadway. He spoke his part in Yiddish, while the rest of the cast spoke English.

American critics came to the Yiddish theater and were delighted. They admitted that the Yiddish theater often inspired the American. Yiddish troupes imported new artistic styles and introduced new European plays. Other ethnic groups in New York—Poles, Germans, Italians, Greeks— also tried to create their own theater. But only the Jews succeeded, perhaps because Jewish audiences received what they deeply desired: broad humanity, rich color, folklore, inspiration, mysticism—a complete escape.

There is a tendency to evaluate the importance of ethnic groups in America in terms of their contribution to the country. It is customary to say the Irish worked as longshoremen, ditchdiggers, construction workers. The Germans introduced scientific farming and shaped the educational system. The Scandinavians turned millions of acres of wilderness into productive land. The Italians were bricklayers and masons and built the cities, skyscrapers, and subways. The Poles were farm laborers, the Greeks planted vineyards, the Chinese built the railroads, the Russians helped develop the mining industry and the factories, the Jews built up the clothing industry and were instrumental in the formation of unions and the development of the movies.

Library shelves are filled with books telling the story of each separate ethnic group that came to this country and contributed to the "developing spirit and betterment" of society. Almost all these books contain lists of names of outstanding personalities which the Irish, the Finns, the Norwegians, or the Hungarians have "given" to this country. John F. Kennedy, in *A Nation of Immigrants,* wrote that "the abundant resources of this land provided the foundation of a great nation, but only people could make the opportunity a reality." He names a number of prominent personalities from various national groups and he pays flattering compliments to the Jewish immigrants.

That method of praising ethnic groups, by calling out the names of their great men, is pleasing. But it also contains its own weakness, and a questionable proposition. For if each Jew and each Italian has a right to collective pride because of "his" David Sarnoff or "his" Enrico Fermi, the same logic places collective responsibility for such characters as Meyer Lansky and Al Capone on every Jew or every Italian. The real contribution of each group lies not in the constellation of glittering individual names, but in the collective human experience, of collective hopes, beliefs, joys and, inevitably, disappointments and sorrows. The great masses of immigrants craving freedom made an imprint on the pattern of the American spirit; the multiplicity of imported religions became the foundation for religious tolerance; the variety of imported talents and skills shaped the material and intellectual life of this country. Millions of separate dreams, brought across the Atlantic, became the ingredients of what is called the "American Dream." The anonymous Jewish immigrant has added his ideas and life-style: a hunger for education, a sense of social justice and intellectual restlessness.

The reception centers of Castle Garden and Ellis Island have become memorials to the past. Gone are the pushcarts from Hester Street, the fantastic theaters on Second Avenue. Almost gone are the strange and beautiful sounds of Yiddish. The life of the Eastern European Jews has already become history to their children, and prehistory to the present generation.

The children of the pushcart peddlers, seltzer vendors, sweatshop jobbers and pressers, have become lawyers, physicians, scholars, playwrights, movie moguls, industrialists, judges, senators, and union leaders. The Old Country, which was carried in the steerage of grim ships and went through the pain and excitement of adaptation, is now deeply embedded in American life. Differences still exist, but they are part of the mosaic which, in the words of Walt Whitman, is a "Nation of Nations."

There still are some who would call life in the shtetl parochial and its continuity in this country narrow ethnicity. But perhaps the opposite is true. The more secular and "broader" the outlook, the more faded and diluted becomes the view, blinding the observer to an experience which has the richness of emotion and the delight of curiosity and wonder.

THE NEW COUNTRY

Above: A New Year postcard shows a postman arriving in a shtetl cottage with money sent from relatives in America.

AMERICA IN THE SHTETL

When the situation of the Jews in East Europe became most desperate, with growing political persecutions and economic pressures, a new hope suddenly exploded in the midst of the Jewish shtetl. The market places and shuls began reverberating with the magic word *America.*

Unlike the Old Messiah who was to deliver the Children of Israel from their bondage and who had tarried so long, the New Messiah, America, was real, waiting at the port of New York, holding out a torch, inviting all who were poor, tired, and yearning to be free.

Sholem Aleichem
A LULLABY

Sleep my child, my joy, my treasure,
Sleep my little one.
Sleep my crown, my only comfort,
Sleep my pretty son. . . .

In America Jews are wealthy
Poverty is rare—
Chicken broth I'll cook you daily
All are equal there.

Translated by Alter Brody

56

Opposite: In the Polish town of Pultusk a group of beggars
celebrate at a party paid for by money sent from America. Above:
Two representatives from the Hebrew Immigrant Aid Society (the
woman in the print dress and the man behind her) pay a visit
to relatives in the old country.

Opposite: The grave of an American Jew who died in Poland and was mistakenly buried in a Christian cemetery is opened so that the body can be buried properly. Below: The Schwartz family of Grzymalow, Galicia, pose for a group portrait, holding up photographs of absent relatives who have already emigrated to America.

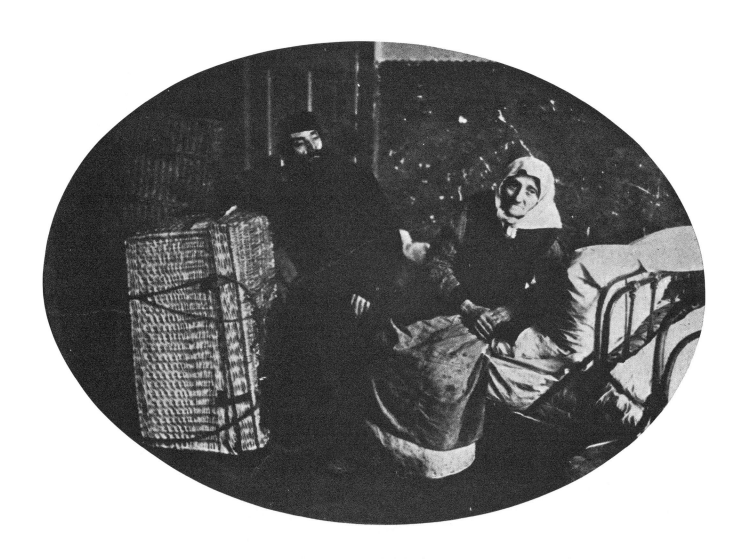

Above: Two elderly emigrants, their belongings wrapped in a straw
hamper, en route to America where they will join their children.

THE EXODUS

The great wave of emigration of the East European Jews to America, at the turn of the century, has often been compared to the biblical Exodus from Egypt. But apart from the fact that here, too, an entire people escaped from a land of slavery, the comparison is not completely correct.

The exodus from Eastern Europe was not accompanied by miracles; the Jews did not leave with "accumulated riches," the sea did not "behold and flee," there was no Moses to guide them.

Abraham Reisin
ON A STRANGE BOAT . . .

On a strange boat
To a strange land came we;
A strange captain guided us
Across the sea.

The boat rocked us back and forth
And those whom she rocked to sleep—
Dreamt heavy dreams,
Heavy dreams and deep. . . .

Translated by Goldie Morgentaler

Above: Lined up at the American consulate in
Warsaw, emigrants wait for a visa. Below: Police
were sometimes required to maintain order
in the waiting line. Opposite: At the Hebrew
Immigrant Aid Society in Warsaw, Jews seeking
visas are assisted by representatives.

63

Below: At a railroad station in Danzig, Jews wait for a train that will take them to their port of embarkation, most likely Hamburg or Bremen. Opposite: Women on their way to join husbands already in America

A pair of rare photographs, above and opposite, shows a party
of Jews attempting to flee across the border between Russia
and Austria—and being apprehended by border guards.
Opposite, at bottom: In 1914, in an immigrants' hostel in Germany, Jews line up for a kosher meal.

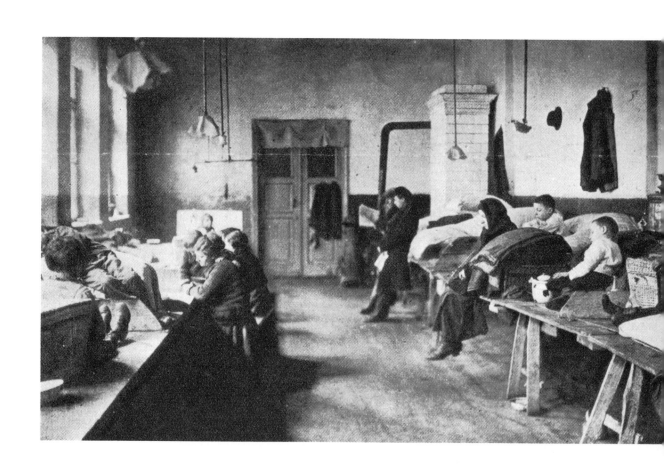

Opposite, top: A hostel dormitory. Opposite, bottom: At Danzig, en route to America, a group of emigrants poses around a table in a Jewish shelter. Below: A family with no chance of coming to America photographed beneath a line of washing hung out to dry.

For most of the emigrants, as for the ones above photographed in Latvia, the route led across Germany and then by ships from one of the major ports. But for some Jews, like the Novikoff family, opposite, who fled Ekaterinoslav in Russia after a pogrom and were photographed in front of the pyramids and Sphinx in Egypt, the route was more roundabout. The Novikoff family eventually settled in Lincoln, Nebraska.

Above: The first sight immigrants had of America was of the officials who processed the incoming throngs.

ARRIVAL

The arrival in the New Country was a shattering experience.
Before stepping down onto the streets "paved with gold,"
the immigrants had to go through the purgatory of the
"reception centers" at Castle Garden and later Ellis Island,
which they called "the Island of Tears."

Sometimes it seemed to them that, despite the great
promise of the wonderland, America, the Statue of Liberty
which greeted the "huddled masses" had a heart made
of bronze also.

I. I. Schwartz
WONDERLAND . . .

America, my wonderland,
My ever young and shiny land,
How beautiful, how vast you are,
How powerful, how strong!

This land of liberty and joy
With truth and justice everywhere,
Where in the hearts of everyone
Resounds the freedom song.

Translated by Moishe Rosenfeld

Opposite: During the voyage across the ocean the deck provided a welcome change from the horrors of the immigrants' steerage accommodations. Above: A crowd of passengers aboard an immigrant ship.

Below: Immigrants within sight of the Statue of Liberty. Opposite, top: Ellis Island. Opposite, bottom: On April 28, 1913, Jewish immigrants who, for one reason or other, had to remain on Ellis Island, celebrate a Passover Seder.

Pages 78-79: The ornate buildings at Ellis Island sheltered a vast reception hall where the immigrants were processed.

For most immigrants the first full view of American life came
on the crowded streets of the Lower East Side, above.

THE NEW LAND

The New Land was not "paved with gold." It was composed of slums, a maze of streets overshadowed by gloomy tenement houses, prison-like buildings with narrow doors, cramped passages, and steep staircases. Entire streets were turned into markets with hundreds of pushcarts.

Abraham Reisin
THE TENEMENT HOUSE

A family of eight
And beds only two—
When the night comes
What do they do?

Three sleep with father,
Three with their mother;
Little hands and feet
Entwined with each other. . . .

It's well known,
That a grave is narrow—
But one sleeps alone.

Translated by Jack Noskovitch

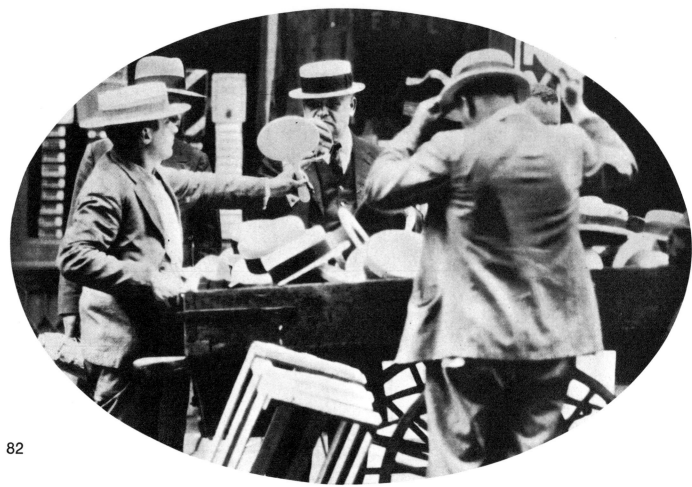

Opposite, top: A Jewish immigrant rests during a hot spell in a Lower East Side park. Opposite, bottom: Old clothing styles were abandoned as a straw hat peddler on Orchard Street does a brisk business. Below: Immigrants dressed in American style.

Opposite and below: Hester Street and Suffolk Street provide bargains in clothes, dishes, and food, all sold from pushcarts. At the time a few wooden houses survived on Hester Street.

Some immigrants, like
S. Levy, managed to
graduate from a pushcart
to a store.

Opposite: A Hasidic rabbi and his beadle stroll down a street in Far Rockaway. This page: Three scenes at Coney Island.

Coney Island (top pictures, both pages) and adjoining Sea Gate
whose gate is opposite, at bottom, became Jewish enclaves.
Below: The more prosperous could afford a trip northward from New
York to take the waters at Saratoga Springs.

Above: Among the many courses provided by the Educational Alliance on the Lower East Side were classes at which adults could learn English and girls could learn cooking. Some knowledge of English was required before the immigrant could join the throngs at the courthouses seeking to take out citizen papers. Opposite, top: A crowd at the Bronx County Court.

Citizens enjoyed the privilege of political participation. Left: In Harlem, where some of the more affluent immigrants moved from the Lower East Side, an immigrant named Jacob Bashein has the chance to shake hands with Theodore Roosevelt himself.

93

At a pageant presented by
the Milwaukee Branch of the
Poale Zion, a labor Zionist
organization, a girl playing
the Statue of Liberty and
a boy playing Abraham
Lincoln proclaim the virtues
of America. The girl,
Goldie Mabowitz, better
known as Golda Meir, later
emigrated to Palestine.

The Wanderer
finds Liberty
in America

In New York, and across the country, Jewish immigrants soon concentrated in separate neighborhoods and eventually in vast quarters of the cities. Above: The first Jewish hotel in the United States, on Delancey Street in New York. In Brownsville, a section of Brooklyn, opposite, more modest buildings are erected to house the expanding Jewish population.

As prosperity and confidence increased, the Jewish presence in the country became more evident with the growth of institutions. Opposite, top: Yeshiva University in New York. Opposite, bottom: Beth Israel Hospital in New York, one of the many Jewish hospitals built in cities across the country to provide patients with kosher accommodations, which were unavailable in general hospitals. Left: The new building of the Yiddish newspaper, the *Jewish Daily Forward,* on the Lower East Side. Above: A copy of the newspaper's first issue, April 22, 1897.

100

In 1916, at the funeral of the great Yiddish writer Sholem Aleichem, an enormous crowd gathers in front of the writer's Bronx apartment house and follows his coffin in a procession through the city streets, opposite. Sholem Aleichem's grave at the Workmen's Circle Cemetery in Brooklyn, above, is next to that of Meyer London, who was a Socialist congressman from the Lower East Side, and close to that of the Yiddish poet Morris Rosenfeld.

Above: Fire hydrants did not exist in the shtetl. They were particularly welcome to Jewish children in the hot, sticky city slums.

CHILDREN

While the parents were bitterly struggling with the harsh conditions of life—toiling in sweatshops, selling from pushcarts, or peddling from door to door—they had one great consolation: the children.

Here, unlike in the Old Country, the opportunities for the children were limitless: the high schools and universities stood open for the sons and daughters of the poor as well as of the rich. But this in turn deepened the gap between the "green" parents and their Americanized children.

Morris Rosenfeld
MY LITTLE SON

I have a son, a little son,
A youngster mighty fine!
When I look at him I feel
That all the world is mine.

But seldom do I see him when
He's wide awake and bright.
I always find him sound asleep;
I see him late at night.

The time-clock drags me off at dawn,
At nights it lets me go.
I hardly know my flesh and blood;
His eyes I hardly know . . .

Translated by Aaron Kramer

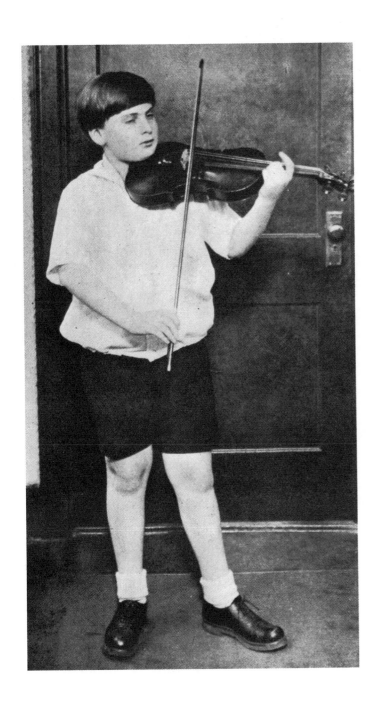

Most immigrant children, like Sammy Goldman, opposite, top, a newsboy in Kitchener, Ont., spent more time on work than at play. There was play, however, even on the slum streets. Opposite, bottom: A damp game of ring-around-a-rosy on Eldridge Street on the Lower East Side. Yehudi Menuhin, left, was the model for many children; violin or piano lessons for children were the first luxuries the immigrants allowed themselves.

Under the direction of the musician Leo Liov, the chorus of the Workmen's Circle—immigrants themselves or the children of immigrants—sang traditional Yiddish folk songs along with proletarian anthems.

At the Baron Hirsch schools run for immigrants by the Educational Alliance, as at the public schools, children were taught both patriotic and gymnastic exercises. Above: Children salute the American flag. Opposite: Girls and boys—separate but equal— perform calisthenics.

In time the children came to enjoy a rare luxury: a trip to a summer camp.
Above: An art class at a camp run by the Workmen's Circle, Silver Lake,
near Pawling, N.Y. YMHAs in the cities provided urban recreation. Opposite:
A YMHA glee-club in St. Louis in the early 1920s. One of the members
was Abram Sachar, later the first president of Brandeis University.

111

Above: A boy, leaving for the synagogue
with his grandfather, kisses the mezuzah on
the doorpost of his house. Children, and
lots of them, were the most visible manifesta-
tion of the immigrant family. Opposite: Mr.
and Mrs. E. Gerber of Lynn, Massachusetts,
surrounded by their numerous progeny.

Above: On Hester Street on the Lower East Side, a peddler with his meager stock spread out in front of him waits for a customer.

WORK

Working conditions were harsh. In most apartments the living room also served as a shop where the whole family, children included, toiled for sixteen hours a day, making cigars, sewing knickers, "finishing" bundles.

The conditions in the sweatshops were even worse. And there was always the hovering danger of "slack times."

Morris Rosenfeld
THE SWEATSHOP

So wild is the roar of machines at the sweatshop,
I often forget I'm alive—in that din!
I'm drowned in the tide of the terrible tumult
My ego is slain; I become a machine.

I work and I work, without rhyme without reason—
Produce and produce, and produce without end.
For what? And for whom? I don't know, I don't wonder—
Since when can a whirling machine comprehend?

Translated by Aaron Kramer

Above: On the Lower East Side, a Jewish bakery and a peddler of pretzels. Opposite, top: Zalmen Rubinowitz, the proprietor of the Malden, Mass., Pickle Works, drives his horse and wagon through the streets of a New England textile mill town. Opposite, bottom: On the Lower East Side, a vendor of secondhand clothing, his stock piled on the sidewalk, helps a customer try on a coat.

Selling, often to each other, was a major immigrant occupation. At left: A row of pushcarts and small stores on the Lower East Side.

For the Jews of New York the garment industry was the employer which kept the community alive. On the streets of the Lower East Side a common sight: workers carrying bundles of unfinished garments home to their tenements to be finished.

Within the tenement workshops, the entire family, children included, work long hours sewing garments.

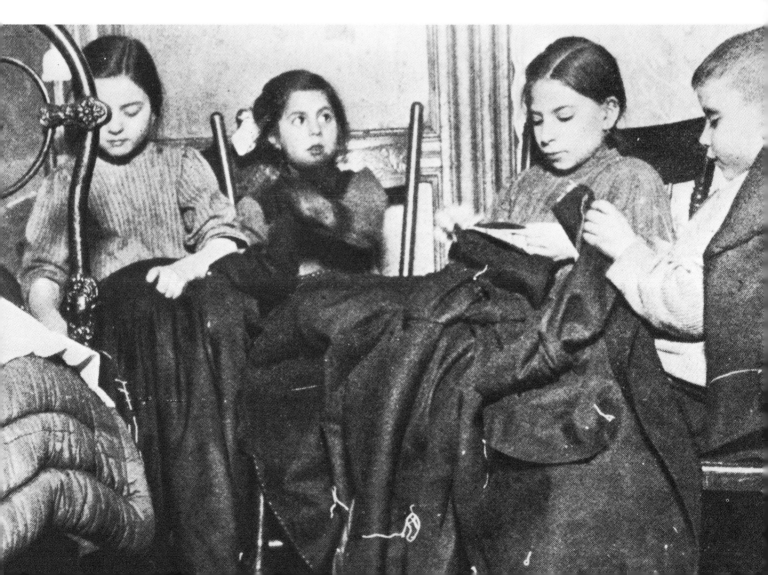

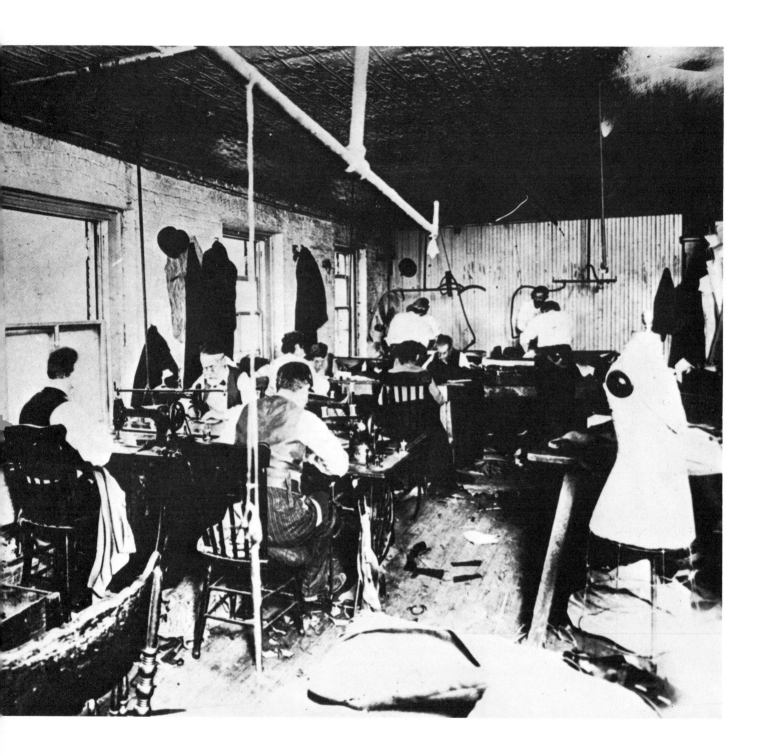

Opposite: Working conditions in lofts where garments were sewn were hardly better then those in the tenement workshops. Workers, above, at a Philadelphia sweatshop earned as little as a dollar for an eighty-hour week.

The struggle to organize garment workers was long and bitter. Below: Shirtwaist makers vote to strike in New York in 1909. Opposite, top: Striking ladies' garment workers in Toronto carry placards or wear sashes proclaiming their cause. Opposite, bottom: The cast of a benefit theatrical group in St. Louis, putting on a benefit performance for striking Cleveland garment workers, poses for a group picture.

Within the unions, bitter partisanship developed. Opposite, bottom: A throng of workers demonstrate against Communist influence in the unions in front of the ILGWU building. Opposite, top: At an outdoor rally, garment workers carry a sign saying, "Our leaders say this strike has been settled, but this demonstration shows otherwise." Below: Samuel Gompers, president of the AFL, addresses a garment workers' rally at Cooper Union in New York.

Above: At the Orthodox Home for the Aged in Chicago, Barnet
Kaufman, a centenarian, practices blowing the *shofar*.

HOLIDAYS

The tempo of life in the New Country made it impossible
to devote all one's time to God. Everything had to be
shortened: the time for serving God, the beard, the length
of the coat. But in the midst of the constant turmoil the
immigrant managed to separate the ordinary days of the
week from the Sabbath and to celebrate the holidays with
the solemnity of the Old Country.

I. I. Schwartz
SABBATH CANDLES

Light your mother's candlestick
At the window, that the shine
Should be seen, and holy Sabbath
May the whole world illumine.

Let your child cling to your apron
With his head against you hid—
Lift your hands and bless the candle
Just as your old mother did.

Translated by J. Leftvitch

Opposite: Housewives shop for the Jewish holidays as they did in the Old Country. Below: Immigrants and their children cast crumbs into the East River in New York symbolically casting their sins away at the New Year.

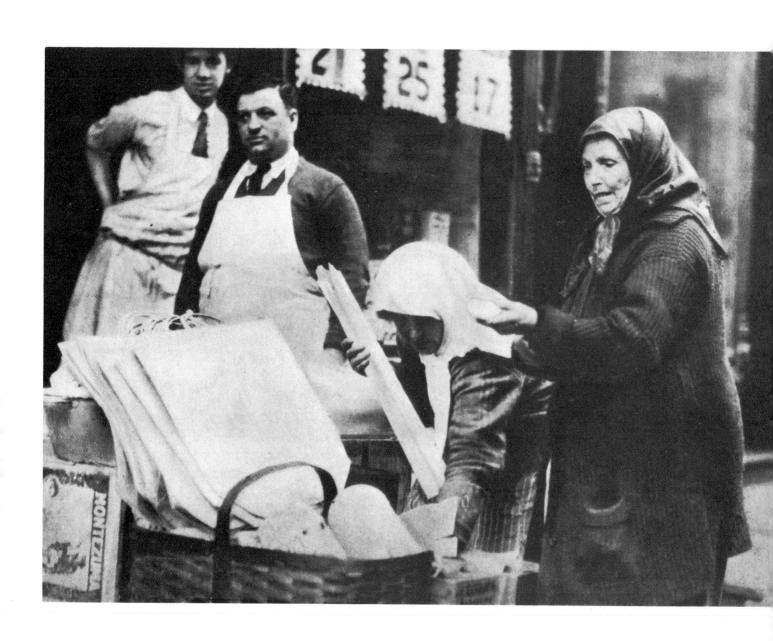

In preparation for Yom Kippur, Jews on the Lower East Side
purchase memorial candles, opposite, and prayer books, above,
from pushcart vendors of religious goods.

At Yom Kippur a rooster or a hen is slaughtered as part of the ancient *kaporoth* custom, in which the animal serves as a substitute for the sins of the worshiper. Below: A woman purchases a hen. Opposite: A man examines a rooster for purchase.

137

At Succoth, palm fronds, below, and citrons, opposite, were purchased by the pious in compliance with the biblical injunction, "And ye shall take you on the first day the boughs of goodly trees, branches of palm trees and the boughs of thick trees and willows of the brook; and ye shall rejoice before the Lord, your God, seven days."

Amid the tenements of their city slums, Jewish immigrants erected
the traditional tabernacles for the feast of Succoth. Opposite,
top: A man covers a *succah* with straw. Opposite, bottom: *Succoth*
in back of tenements on the Lower East Side. Below: A woman
sets a table inside a New York *succah.*

Although these photographs were taken in New York, they could have been taken in shtetls of Eastern Europe. Below: A baker prepares *matzoth* for Passover. Opposite: A tinsmith scours pans to make sure they are clean for the Passover holiday.

The Passover Seder, important enough in the Old Country, became one of the most important manifestations of Jewish identity in the New. People put on their best clothes for the occasion. Below: The Oberman family of New York. Opposite: The Harry Leon family of Chicago.

Right: The sounding of the *shofar.* Above: New Year greeting cards could be purchased from pushcarts on the Lower East Side. Opposite, upper left: A child with his grandparents. Upper right: A heart being weighed against gold; the card says "Money means nothing, the heart is finer." Bottom: A festive holiday meal, for men only.

146

לשנה טובה תכתבו
חבקוד בשבת

לשנה טובה תכתבו
A happy New Year

וועגט דער מלאך הארץ און געלד, —
זיי זעע נישט גענארם.
געלד איז בלאסע שבבלאטע,
דהארץ בלייבט תמיד צארם.

לשנה טובה תכתבו

A Happy New Year

New Year greeting cards manufactured in Europe but sold in America to Yiddish-speaking immigrants show, top, a family meal and, at bottom, a pious man giving charity, while his son looks on and, it is to be hoped, learns from him.

לשנה טובה תכתבו

A happy New Year

טראגט זיך דאָס שיפעל צום גאָלדענעם ברעג,
צום ליכטיגען ניי־יאָהר, צ' זוניגע טעג.
צאָפלען זיך הערצליך, פליסט הייסער דאָס בלוט,
חערט אזוי זיס, אזוי ליעבליך און גוט.

Above: A romantic American scene. The caption of the picture reads, "Boat, take us to the golden shore, to a shining New Year, to sunny days. Our hearts are fluttering, our blood flows warm." Left: A more subdued excursion—a trip to the synagogue.

149

Above: An immigrant named Hyman Levy spent his old age in Richmond, Va.

OLD AGE

In the old country old age was surrounded with respect.
Families were tightly knit units; they included the grandparents, who were the object of esteem and pride. In the
early days of immigration many grandparents, following
the custom of the shtetl, remained with their children
and grandchildren. But very soon the widespread custom
of sending the old to old age homes began to prevail.

Abraham Reisin
HOW OLD?

You ask me how old am I today;
I'd tell you my years if I could,
But trust me, friend, I myself cannot say;
To count them would not be good.

If life means to suffer, I've lived a long time,
My years have been plenty on earth;
If life means that joy lets us thrill to her chime,
Then I'm still awaiting my birth.

Translated by Aaron Kramer

Sarah Lapidus, A. Rochinger, Hannah Ront, Hirsch Borenfeld, and Alta Elfand all lived to be a hundred in the New World. The photograph of them, below, was taken in a home for the aged in Brooklyn. Opposite: Joseph and Molly Solomon, married in the Old Country, are shown hugging each other on their fiftieth anniversary in the New.

153

Opposite: In 1922, the Association of Immigrants from the city of Bialystok dedicates the Bialystoker Home for the Aged on the Lower East Side. Below: Three residents of the Home.

A great many of the old managed to remain with their families as they would have in Europe instead of ending their days in an old age home, according to the widespread American custom. Above: In Brownsville, Brooklyn, an old man shovels snow. Below: Elderly women enjoy the sun in a Lower East Side park. Opposite: An old man purchases a new prayer shawl.

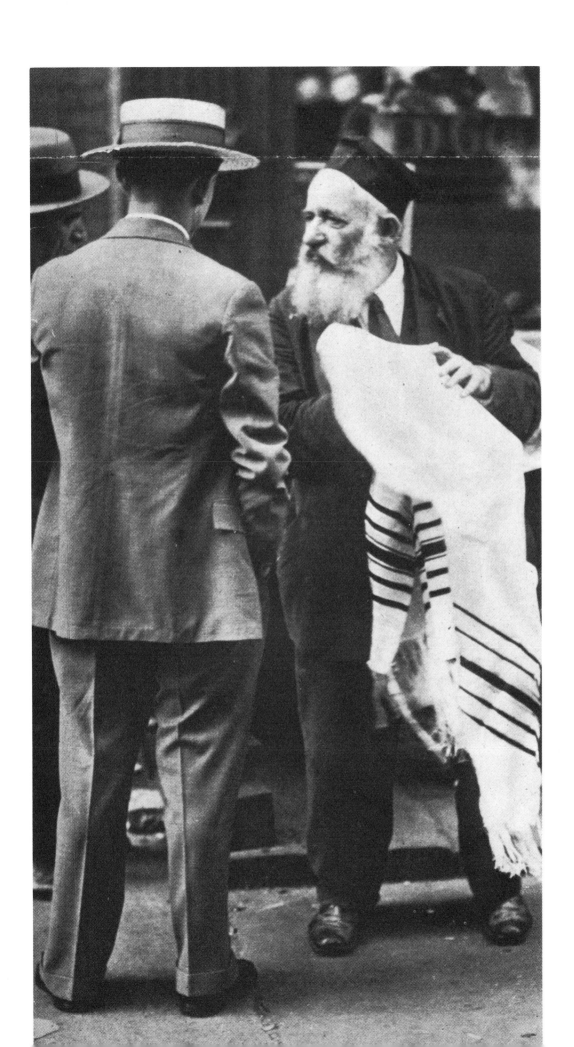

Most Jews kept on working as long as they could. For immigrants it was poor health, not old age, that forced retirement. Above: A pretzel vendor and a newsdealer. Opposite: An elderly man on the Lower East Side goes out to a synagogue.

Above: At the Hebrew Home for the Aged in the Dorchester section of Boston, bearded residents line up for a group portrait on the front steps. Opposite: Inside the building, men study the Talmud.

161

162

Opposite: An old age home class picture, taken in New York.
Below: Four generations of one Brooklyn family, Gershon Dreisin
poses with his great-grandson Lawrence Luber, along with his
daughter and granddaughter.

Above: Two actors appearing in an operetta called *Parisian Love* at one of the Second Avenue Yiddish theaters.

THEATER

For most immigrants Yiddish theater was not just a matter
of amusement; it was a fulfillment of their cultural needs.
The theater gave them comedies and dramas about the
miseries of immigrants' life and at the same time allowed
them to be nostalgic about the shtetl. Many other ethnic
groups tried to create their own theaters, but only the
Jews succeeded, perhaps because Jewish audiences
received what they deeply desired: a complete escape.

LONG LIVE COLUMBUS*

Wars and guns and flowing blood
We need like a hole in the head.
The governor—his name is mud,
The Czar should only be dead.
We are free, we are free—
So sing along with me:

Long live Columbus,
Drink up, brothers, l'chaim!
Long live Columbus!
All the Jews should try him.

It's great and it's wonderful
For the humble and pompous—
Long live Columbus!
Long live Columbus!

Translated by Moishe Rosenfeld

*This was one of the most popular songs
of the Yiddish Second Avenue theater.

דער גרויסער מאמענט!

MAX GABEL . JE... ...GOLDSTEIN

GREAT MOMENT

Beginning TUESDAY MAT. SEPT 11

EVERY FRIDAY — SAT. & SUN.

דער גרויסער מאמענט!

The Great Moment,
starring the well-known
actress Jenny Goldstein,
was such a popular
feature that crowds lining
up for tickets in front of
Gabel's Second Avenue
Theater had to be turned
away.

Above: A theater advertisement
—in English—from a Yiddish
newspaper. Opposite: A Knoxville,
Tenn., patriarch Guntel Bart, who
claimed to be 108 years old, was
photographed attending the
Yiddish theater along with his
descendants during a trip to
New York.

169

Scenes from the Yiddish theater. Opposite, top: Aaron Lebedieff and Bessie Weisman in *Mendel from Japan.* Opposite, bottom: Six geishas from the same play. Above: A scene from a melodrama entitled *The First Bride.* Below: An extravaganza from *Parisian Love.*

Theatrical troupes traveled to the major Jewish settlements outside New York. Opposite, top: The Anshel Shor troupe in Philadelphia, in 1913. Shor is shown at the center in the first row. Sholem Asch was a popular playwright as well as a novelist. Opposite, bottom: A scene from his classic play *Motke the Thief.* Above: Two dashing matinee idols in a play called *Caucasian Love.*

Among the well-known Yiddish actors in the American theater were Leon Golubok, center at left, who came to America with the first agricultural settlers in the 1880s; Maurice Schwartz (second from right, below), and David Kessler (next to him), who are shown in a scene from *Yankel Boyle;* and the young Molly Picon, opposite.

Above: A Jewish family named Handelman rides in an open wagon across the South Dakota plains.

AGRICULTURAL SETTLEMENTS

Some Jewish immigrants, most of them young people from the Russian cities of Kiev and Odessa, came to the New Country with the idea of becoming farmers; to "show the world" by building agricultural settlements according to the teachings of ancient prophets and the new teachings of Rousseau and Leo Tolstoy that Jews could be more than tailors and peddlers.

Alas, the romanticism of the young idealists ended, in almost all cases, in failure.

Eliyokum Zunser
IN THE PLOW . . .

In the plow
My fortune grows,
Life's true joy and bliss—
Nothing is amiss. . . .

I have as much as I need
My household to feed.
And as I sow and reap—always
The Lord God I praise.

Translated by Moishe Rosenfeld

Above: Jews who settled in Kansas in 1885 lived in houses made of sod blocks cut out of the prairie. Opposite, top: A lithograph dating from around the same period shows a flourishing Jewish farming village in Burleigh County along the upper reaches of the Missouri River in what is now North Dakota. Opposite, bottom: A Jewish tobacco farmer.

ריע רוססי ש ידישע פארמער קאלאני וועקסלער אין ראקארא אין אבעריקא

DRAWN FROM NATURE BY S LEVY

THE RUSSIAN JEWISH FARMER SETTLEMENT WECHSLER
BURLEIGH COUNTY — DAKOTA TERRITORY.

Jewish agricultural settlements survived well into the twentieth century. Below: Young farmers armed with rakes, shovels, and pitchforks at one of the agricultural settlements sponsored by the Baron de Hirsch funds. Opposite: A dairy farmer at a Jewish agricultural settlement in Oklahoma.

Above: Four generations of a Detroit Jewish family. Left to right: Evelyn Kalman; her mother; her grandmother, Sarah Kapetansky; and her great-grandmother, Bella Zlotchenko.

FAMILY ALBUM

The early years of the Eastern Jewish immigrants have already become history to their children, and prehistory to the present generation. Gone are the pushcarts from Hester Street, the fantastic theaters on Second Avenue. The Old Country, which was carried in the steerage of grim ships and went through the pain of adaptation, is now deeply imbedded in American life.

What remains of this vanished past are the faded leaves in the Family Album.

M. L. Halpern
ON THE SHORES OF THIS
BEAUTIFUL LAND

You and I—children of another world—
We have on the shores of this beautiful land
Constructed our abode.
We have wandered long and arrived late, so late,
Only free and great remains the shore—
And tomorrow, tomorrow new cities will be built
And the sky will hang so fair over us
And the days, so white, will become long, so long.

Translated by Moishe Rosenfeld

Three more family groups of four generations. Above, right to left: Chaya Bellsman, eighty-five; Eva Silver, sixty-five; Anna Schneiderman, thirty; and Dora Schneiderman, ten. Opposite, top: Koppel Cooper; his son Morris; grandson Harry; and great-grandson Stanley, of Brooklyn. Opposite, bottom: Mrs. C. Mayerson of San Francisco, with her son, grand-daughter, and great-grandson.

Opposite: An expert who specialized in installing fringes on old prayer shawls on the Lower East Side. Below: Eight children of Samuel Wiener of Hammond, Indiana.

188

Left: Mr. and Mrs. Julius Winick of Massachusetts, with their children, grandchildren, and other members of their family. Below: The Wishnow family of Boston.

Opposite, top: Leyb Hirsch Goldstein, one of the founders of the Rumanian synagogue on Rivington Street on the Lower East Side, shown along with his wife. Above: An elegantly dressed couple, unidentified, of New York. Left: A Passover Seder; the family is unidentified.

Above: An elderly Jewish man of the Bronx. Opposite:
A cantor and his granddaughter, a student at the
University of Chicago.

194

Opposite: A street merchant selling vegetables on the Lower East Side. Below: A talk between two East Side grandmothers.

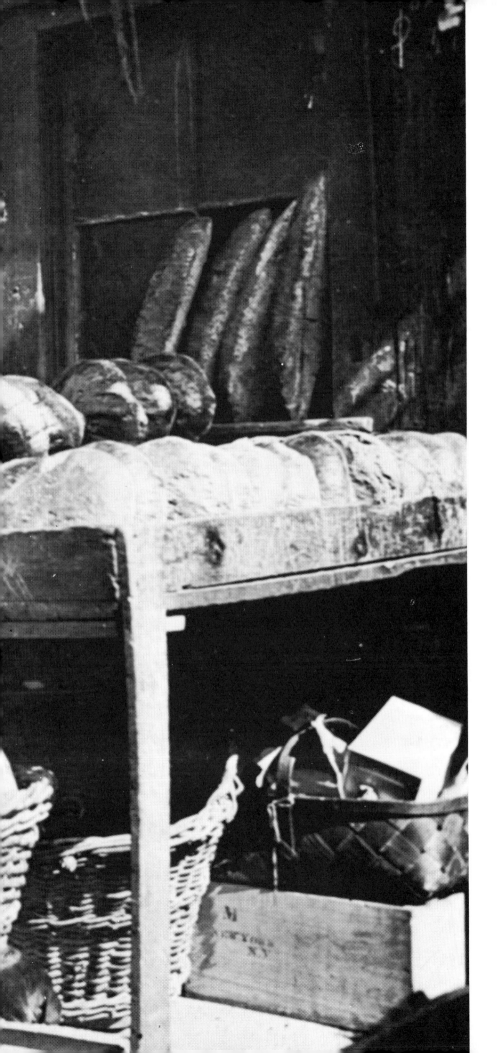

Selling bread
in New York.

Right: Mrs Toba Feiga Grossman, formerly of Pozelva, Lithuania, photographed in St. Louis with her son, grandchild, and great-grandchild. Opposite: Four New England women: Sarah Berkowitz of Providence, R.I.; Bessie Kadish of New Bedford, Mass.; Lilian and Estella Stein.

Left: Abraham Cahan, editor-in-chief and one of the founders of the *Jewish Daily Forward.* Opposite: A group of famous Yiddish poets, who formed a group called *In Zikh,* "Intro-spect." The poets who posed for this photo in 1923 are Jacob Glatstein, B. Alquit, M. Licht, J. Stodolski, Celia Dropkin, A. Glanz-Leyeles, and N. B. Minkoff.

Opposite: Mr. and Mrs. Abraham Moses Abramson of Brooklyn.
Below: Eighty-eight-year-old, white-bearded Samuel Kite of
Chicago, formerly of Lodovka, Russia, and his family.

204

Above: A group of traveling actors, members of a road company in America in 1911. Seated in the second row (second from left) is Clara Young, who later became a world-famous folk singer. Opposite: The Workmen's Circle mandolin orchestra of Hartford, Conn., composed of children of members of the organization.

Below: The annual meeting of the Mother's Club for Dental and Medical Aid at Madison House on New York's Lower East Side. Opposite: Jewish boys on their way home from school.

207

Budding American capitalists: Jewish youngsters in Brooklyn,
inspired by the heat, selling homemade lemonade.